2

D0501140

SCIENCE WORKSHOP

SOUND · NOISE & MUSIC

Mick Seller

GLOUCESTER PRESS

NEW YORK CHICAGO LONDON SYDNEY

Design	David West
	Children's Book Design
Designer	Steve Woosnam-Savage
Editor	Suzanne Melia
Picture Researcher	Emma Krikler
Illustrators	Ian Moores
	Ian Thompson
Consultant	Bryson Gore

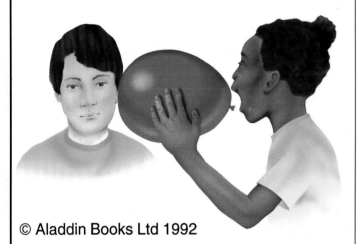

First published in
the United States in 1993 by
Gloucester Press
95 Madison Avenue
New York, NY 10016

Library of Congress Cataloging-in-Publication Data

Seller, Mick.
  Sound, noise, and music / Mike Seller.
    p.   cm. — (Science workshop)
  Includes index.
  Summary: Suggests experiments and projects for
exploring the properties and principles of sound
waves and how they can produce noise or music.
  ISBN 0-531-17408-5
  1. Sound-waves—Juvenile literature. 2. Sound-
waves—Experiments—Juvenile literature. [1.
Sound—Experiments. 2. Experiments.] I. Title. II.
Series.
QC243.2.S45   1993
  534'.078—dc20   92-33923   C IP   AC

CONTENTS

PHOTOCREDITS

All the photographs in this book are by Roger
Vlitos apart from pages; 10 top: Robert
Harding Picture Library; 14 top, 22 top & 24
top: Spectrum Colour Library; 18 top: British
Broadcasting Corporation.

INTRODUCTION

In science, sound is a form of energy, like light or heat. To us, though, it is many things. It can be the annoying noise of a barking dog, the beautiful music of an orchestra, or the soothing sound of waves on the shore. Sound can travel through most things, whether they are gas, liquid, or solid. However, it cannot travel through space. In air, sound travels out in all directions until it is interrupted by something solid. These solid objects reflect sound, causing echoes. Sounds are formed by vibrating objects. For example, your vocal chords when you sing, a guitar string when you pluck it, and a drum when you bang it, all have vibrating parts. These vibrations cause sound waves which travel through the air at about 1,100 feet per second to reach our ears. Some sounds are too high for people to hear, but can be picked up by many animals like bats or dogs. Some sounds are too low to hear, but we may still feel their vibrations. Babies still in the womb can hear sounds, whales in the sea can hear sounds carried through the water, and grasshoppers hear sounds through ears situated on their knees! People who cannot hear sounds may use special hearing aids to help them.

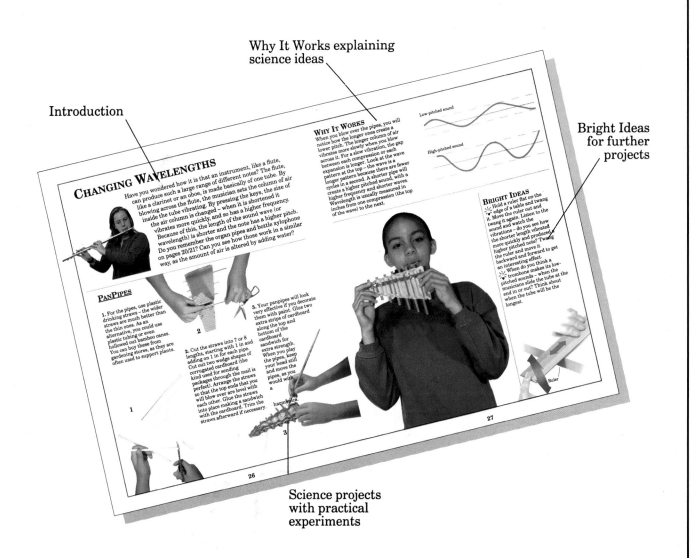

Why It Works explaining science ideas

Introduction

Bright Ideas for further projects

Science projects with practical experiments

THE WORKSHOP

A science workshop is a place to test ideas, perform experiments, and make discoveries. To prove many scientific facts, you don't need a lot of fancy equipment. In fact, everything you need for a basic workshop can be found around your home or school. Read through these pages, and then use your imagination to add to your "home laboratory." As you work your way through this book, you should enjoy completing the projects and seeing your models work. Remember though that from a scientific point of view, these projects are just the starting point. For example, when you finish making the guitar on pages 14 and 15, ask your own questions like "What would happen if I tighten the strings?" "Would thicker strings give higher or lower notes?" and so on. Also, by sharing ideas, you will learn more. Experimenting with equipment, as well as with ideas, will give you the most accurate results. In this way you will build up your workshop as you go along.

MAKING MODELS

Before you begin, read through all the steps. Then make a list of the things you need and gather them together. Next, think about the project so that you have a clear idea of what you are about to do. Finally, take your time in putting the pieces together. You will find that your projects work best if you wait while glue or paint dries. If something goes wrong, retrace your steps. And, if you can't fix it, start over again. Every scientist makes mistakes, but the best ones know when to begin again!

SAFETY WARNINGS

Make sure that an adult knows what you are doing at all times. Cutting the top off a plastic bottle can be difficult and dangerous if you use sharp scissors. Ask an adult to do this for you. Always be careful with balloons and plastic bags. Never cover your face with them. If you spill any water, wipe it up straight away. Slippery surfaces are dangerous. Clean up after you have finished.

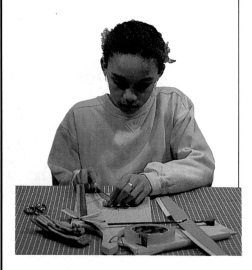

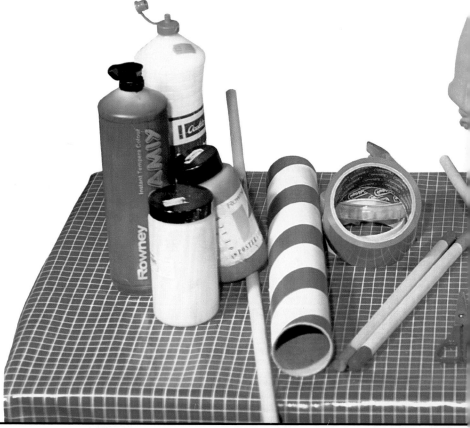

GENERAL TIPS

There are at least two parts to every experiment: experimenting with materials and testing a science "fact." If you don't have all the materials, experiment with others instead. For example if you can't find any glass bottles, use some drinking glasses instead. Once you've finished experimenting, read your notes thoroughly and think about what happened, evaluating your measurements and observations. See what conclusions you can draw from your results.

EXPERIMENTING

Always conduct a "fair test." Only change one thing at a time for each stage of an experiment, so you can always tell which change caused a different result. As you go along, record what you see. Ask questions such as "why?" "how?" and "what if ?" Then test your experiment and write down the answers.

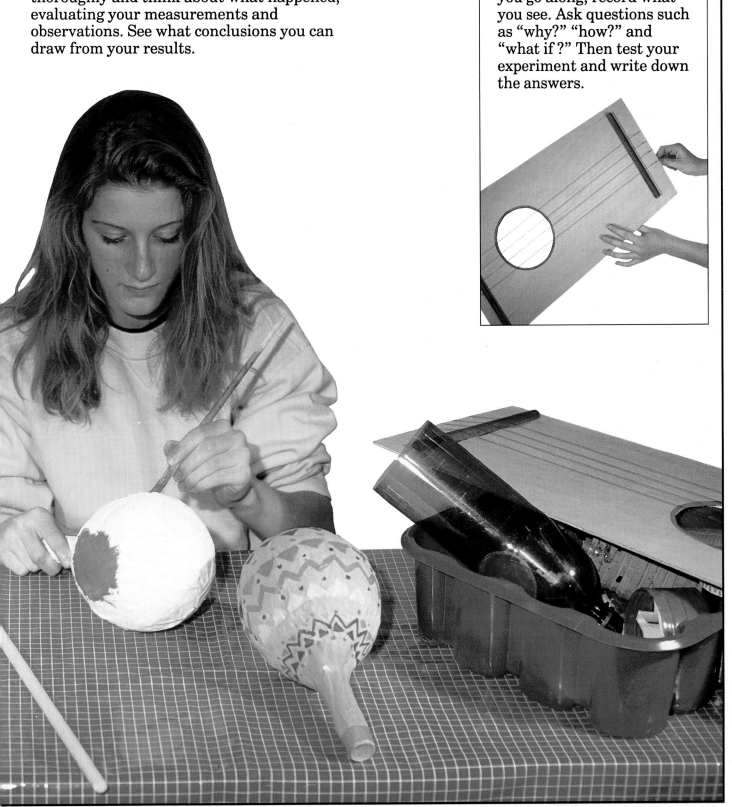

VIBRATIONS

Have you ever thrown a pebble into a pond and watched the ripples spread? The impact of the pebble in the water creates waves – and in a similar way all sounds cause waves in the air. Unlike water waves, sound waves do not move up and down, but travel forward in regions of high and low pressure. Sounds are produced by very fast back and forth movements called vibrations. If you hold your throat lightly a few inches below your chin and talk, you will feel the vibrations. These vibrations produce sound waves in the air by pushing and pulling it to produce pressure changes. We hear the sound when these waves reach our ears. There is no sound on the moon because there is no air to carry the waves.

BEAT THE DRUM

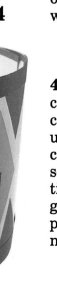

2. Keep the plastic in place with string, or with rubber bands. Pull the polyethylene down to make a tight skin and trim the spare polyethylene away.

1. Stretch a piece of thick polyethylene or plastic over the open top of a pail or large can. A metal pail will be more effective than a plastic one.

3. To give your drum a professional finished look, make a cardboard cover to decorate the outside of it. Make the cover 0.5in taller than your drum and leave 5 in overlap for attaching it on when it is finished.

4. A rectangle of white cardboard is ideal for the cover. Work out a pattern using other colors of cardboard, or you could use scraps of material, paints, felt tip pens, wax crayons etc. The green strips shown above provide a border that gives a neat look to the whole thing.

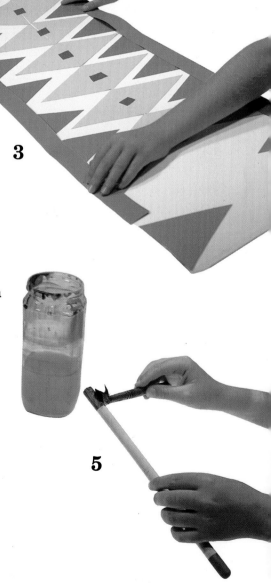

5. Wooden drumsticks are best. Make sure they have rounded ends and finish them off with a touch of paint. Now your drum is ready to play. Remember – don't hit your drum too hard or you will quickly damage the skin.

Compressions

Vibrations

WHY IT WORKS

When you bang the top of the drum, the plastic skin vibrates. As the skin moves up, it pushes against the air and causes a compression, or squashing, of the air above the drum. As it moves down, it compresses the air below the skin, while just above it the air expands to fill the space. As the skin vibrates and moves up again, an expansion is caused below the skin and a new compression takes place above it. One compression and one expansion together is called one cycle. A series of cycles makes a sound wave.

BRIGHT IDEAS

Put sand or grains of rice onto your drum and bang it. Watch the vibrations of the drum's skin make the sand or rice vibrate, too. Does a loud bang make bigger vibrations?

Watch the loudspeakers in a radio or stereo. Can you see them vibrate? Is there a difference when the sound is turned louder?

SOUND WAVES

Sound waves are similar to light waves in some ways. Like a beam of light can be reflected from a mirror, so a sound can be reflected from a surface like a wall. If you shout loudly in your school hall, the sound waves travel to the wall and are bounced back, reaching your ears a split second later – this is an echo. Bats make use of echoes when finding their way, or hunting. They give out a very high pitched sound that bounces back from objects or insects, telling them how far away things are. We can also use this method to find objects that we cannot see. Sonar uses sound to locate objects at the bottom of the sea, such as shipwrecks and shoals of fish.

FIRING WAVES

1. This cannon will send a narrow "beam" of sound waves. Begin by making a pair of wheels for your cannon using circles of cardboard, paper plates, thread spools, and a wooden stick.

1

2. Make a large tube of stiff cardboard for the cannon itself, 18-20 inches in diameter, and four feet long. Make the back of the cannon by covering a circle of cardboard with plastic wrap. Fix it with tape. **2**

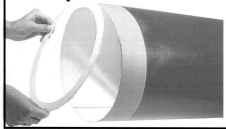

3

3. The front of the cannon is a disk of stiff cardboard with a 1 in hole in the center. You could decorate this with a disk of colored paper.

4

4. Tape the ends of the cannon firmly with double sided tape – this will enable you to fix the ends onto the tube and not into it.

5. Fix the tube to the wheels with tape, and weight the back end of the cannon so that it does not tip forward. Aim the cannon at a wall and tap the plastic wrap quite firmly – from a distance you should get an echo. Make a curtain from 0.5 in strips of foil. Fire your cannon at the curtain. You should see the sound waves making the foil vibrate.

5

WHY IT WORKS

When you strike the piece of plastic wrap (diaphragm) on the cannon, the vibrations lead to sound waves being formed. The waves travel outward from the diaphragm, making the air particles around move back and forth in the same direction. When the waves leaving the front of the cannon meet a solid object, some of them are reflected while some continue traveling through the object, making it move slightly like the air particles. A bat uses sound to find objects in the dark. It produces sounds and then listens for the echoes to be reflected. This is called echolocation.

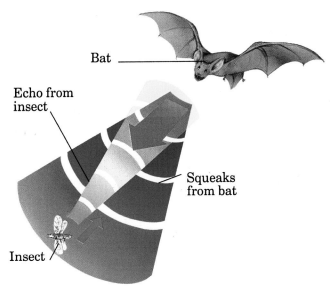

Bat

Echo from insect

Squeaks from bat

Insect

BRIGHT IDEAS

💡 Which surfaces are best for echoing? Can you make an echo in a bathroom, a kitchen, a cafeteria, a hall, a subway? Try other places, too. Do you think hard surfaces are better than soft surfaces for giving echoes? Which sounds echo the best?

💡 Try shouting, knocking two stones together, banging two blocks of wood together, whistling, and talking. Do short, sharp sounds echo better than long soft ones?

💡 The cannon channels the sound waves in one direction. Make a megaphone to channel your voice. Make a narrow cone, and then a wide cone. Shout to a friend through each cone. Shout again, aiming the megaphone 30 feet to their side. What happens? Which cone makes your voice sound louder, and which can you hear best from the side? Can you figure out why?

HOW SOUNDS ARE HEARD

When sound waves enter our ears, they strike the eardrum which vibrates back and forth. This in turn causes tiny bones called ossicles to vibrate. These vibrations are turned by our "inner ear" into electrical signals that pass along nerves to the brain. When the signals reach the brain, we hear sounds. People cannot hear some sounds because they are too high or too low – not everyone can hear the high-pitched squeak of a bat. Dogs can hear higher pitched sounds than people, and a scientist called Sir Francis Galton (1822–1911) invented a whistle for calling dogs which was too high for people to hear. This kind of sound is called ultrasonic sound, or ultrasound.

WHY IT WORKS

The sound waves from your friend's voice make the plastic wrap vibrate. These vibrations are transmitted into your cardboard "ossicles" and can be seen by watching the mirror for movements. This is a simple model of how a real ear works.

Vibrations in the air (sound waves) enter the outer ear and make the eardrum itself vibrate. The three bones, the malleus, the incus, and the stapes, together known as the ossicles, transmit the vibrations through the middle ear to the oval window, or vestibular fenestra. The force of the vibrations on the oval window is over 20 times greater than that of the original vibrations on the eardrum. The oscillations (or vibrations) of the stapes makes the fluid in the part of the inner ear called the cochlea vibrate. The cochlea also contains fibers that pick up the vibrations and send messages along nerves to the brain. Other parts of the ear control our balance – these are called semicircular canals.

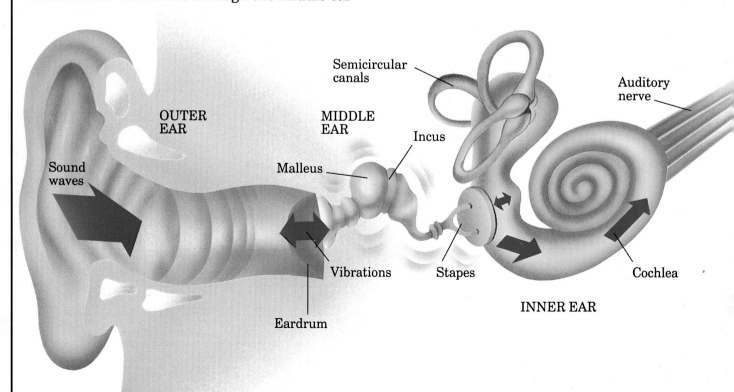

Semicircular canals

Auditory nerve

OUTER EAR

MIDDLE EAR

Incus

Sound waves

Malleus

Vibrations

Stapes

Cochlea

Eardrum

INNER EAR

HEAR THIS?

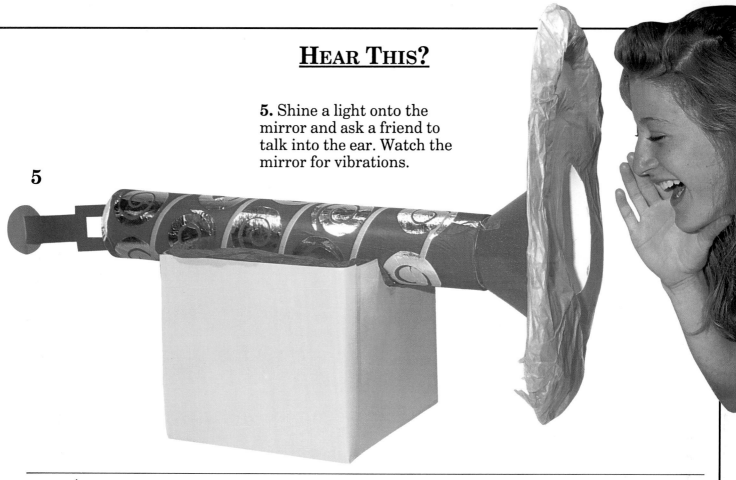

5. Shine a light onto the mirror and ask a friend to talk into the ear. Watch the mirror for vibrations.

5

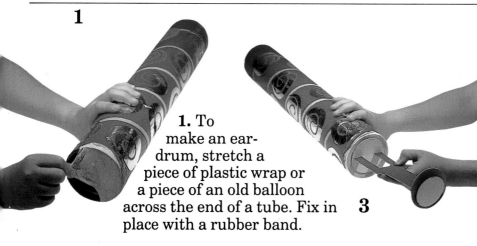

1

1. To make an eardrum, stretch a piece of plastic wrap or a piece of an old balloon across the end of a tube. Fix in place with a rubber band.

2. Make a set of "ossicles" with two disks and a fork shape of thin cardboard held together with double sided tape.

2

4. Make an outer ear from a cone of cardboard with a hole at its end. With careful use of pink tissue paper you can achieve quite a realistic look!

3

3. Attach a small mirror or a disk of shiny foil to one end, and attach the other to the plastic wrap "eardrum" on the tube. Your middle ear is complete.

4

BRIGHT IDEAS

☀ Watch the oval window of your ear again. How does it respond to shouting, whispering, whistling etc? The vibrations of your oval window could be a result of blowing on the eardrum, rather than the vibrations of sound waves. Use a radio to create sound without blowing.

☀ A hundred years ago, people who suffered from hearing loss used ear trumpets. Find out about these devices! Can you make your own?

☀ Listen to sounds blindfolded. Put your hand over one ear and try to tell which direction a sound is coming from. Listen to the same sound with both ears. Can you hear a difference? It is easier to hear the direction of sound with both ears.

TRAVELING SOUNDS

It is not only air that can transmit sound waves. North American Indians knew that the ground itself could carry sound waves, and would listen to the noises of approaching animals and enemies by putting their ears to the ground. Swimmers can hear sound through the water. Whales and dolphins can communicate underwater. Some substances are better transmitters of sound than others, and sound travels faster through some materials, for example steel, than others, like air.

BUILD A TELEPHONE

1. You can make a simple "string telephone" and see how a piece of string transmits sounds. Pierce a small hole in the bottom of a plastic cup with a sharp pencil. Repeat with a second cup.

2. Thread a piece of thin string through the cups and tie several knots in each end of the string. You can decorate your cups by painting them if you want to.

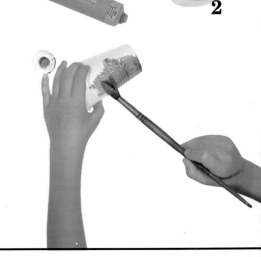

1

2

WHY IT WORKS

When you talk into the plastic cup, your voice makes sound waves that travel through the air. When the vibrations of the air reach the cup, the plastic begins to vibrate in response. Substances that carry sound are called the sound medium. When the string vibrates, it acts as a sound medium, carrying the sound waves to the other cup. Here, the vibrations cause the air inside and around the cup to oscillate, too – carrying the sound to the receiver's ear.

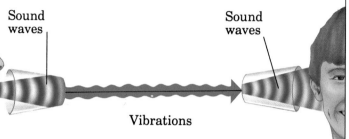

Sound waves

Sound waves

Vibrations

BRIGHT IDEAS

Suspend a long, loose spring, such as a Slinky, on pieces of cotton so that it is hanging horizontally. Tap one end with a spoon. Can you see the vibrations travel along the spring? It is carrying the sound waves and acting as a sound medium.

Put a glass to the wall. Put your ear to the glass. Can you hear noises in the next room? The wall and the glass are acting as sound media.

Ask a friend to bang two stones together in a bucket of water. Listen to the sound through a piece of hose pipe which has one end in the water.

3

3. You will need a friend for the next step. Pull the cups apart so that the string is stretched quite tightly – now you can send a telephone message. If you touch the string while you are talking you will feel the vibrations – but is the message still as clear?

AMPLITUDE AND LOUDNESS

This is an oscilloscope – a machine that can measure sound waves. The louder a sound is, the higher the wave patterns will be from top to bottom. When an object vibrates, the air surrounding it moves back and forth as well (creating a sound wave – see page 6). The distance each particle of air moves from its starting position is called the amplitude of the wave. As loudness depends on a person's ability to hear a sound, scientists cannot really measure loudness. Instead, they measure the energy, or "intensity," of a sound wave. The units they use are decibels.

WHY IT WORKS

When you plucked it gently, the string of the guitar only vibrated a little. During compression, particles of air will move a little way from where they started, and during expansion, they will move back to their original position and a little beyond. On the graph below, imagine that the green line shows where the string or particle of air started, the top of the red line shows how far it moved on compression, and the bottom of the red line shows the same for expansion. The distance from one peak to the next (the red line) is called the wavelength. The distance from the green line to the top of the peak is called the amplitude; the greater the amplitude, the larger the wave.

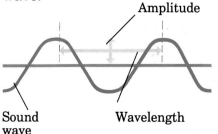

Amplitude

Sound wave   Wavelength

14

STRUMMING AWAY

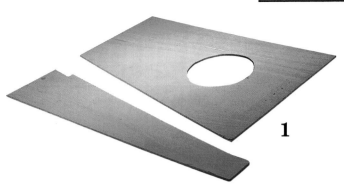

1. You can make your own guitar, but you will need a little help from an adult. Cut a piece of plywood 24 in by 16 in and make a wide hole 6 in from one end. Use sandpaper to remove the rough edges.

2. Ask an adult to cut two pieces of copper pipe or wood dowels, 12 in long. For the strings you can use thin wire or string, but fishing line gives the best results. Cut four or five lengths.

3. Fix the strings to metal eyes screwed into the plywood. If the ends come out on the other side, cover them with a little tape. To give a range of notes, tighten the top strings more than the bottom ones. Note where the copper pipes or wood dowels go.

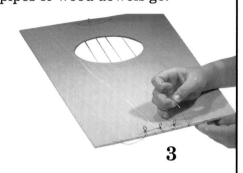

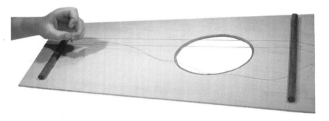

2

4. A soundbox made of cardboard can now be fixed to the back of your guitar. A wooden box, however, gives a better sound quality. Now you are ready to play your guitar!

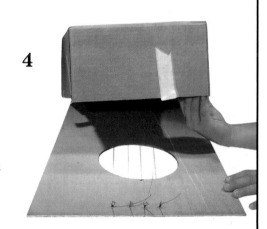

4

BRIGHT IDEAS

Remove the soundbox and listen – is the guitar as loud? Inside the soundbox, the sound waves bounce around (reverberate) before escaping through the hole.

Try a larger or a smaller sound box. Does this make any difference?

Ask a friend to play your guitar and listen to it first from in front, and then from behind. Is there a difference in loudness?

See if you can borrow a tuning fork. Tap the tuning fork on a wooden block (not metal or stone as this will damage it). Listen to the tuning fork. Now tap the tuning fork again and gently hold its base onto different objects, for example, a cookie jar, a table, a cushion, your guitar. The hard objects reverberate more and make the sounds louder than the soft objects.

STOPPING SOUND

Do you like singing in the bath? Somehow your voice can sound more powerful, can't it? This is because the sound waves are reflected off the hard, flat surface of the bathroom walls; the sound "reverberates." In a room like your living room, your voice will sound weaker because the sound is soaked up by the drapes and the furniture. In a recording studio, the engineers have to be very careful not to have too much reverberation, but not to have too dead a sound either. They also soundproof the walls to keep the sounds in!

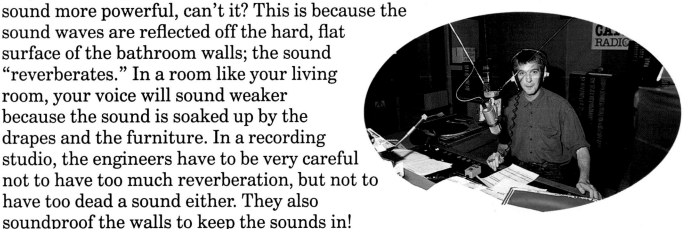

SOUNDPROOFING

1

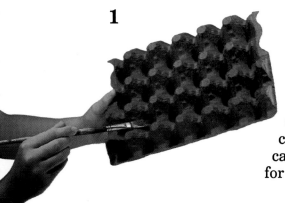

1. You can make a soundproof box to give the same effect as an insulated recording studio. Begin by collecting five or six old cardboard cartons used for storing eggs.

3

3. Cut the egg cartons carefully to size so that they fit neatly and exactly into the inside of the box. Line the bottom and all four walls with the boxes, saving one for the top.

2. Find an old cardboard box that is in good condition with its lid intact. Line the four walls and the bottom of the box with a thick soft material, for example, old dish towels.

4. When you have done this, make sure all your linings are held in securely. Next, prepare the top insulation of egg carton and cloth.

2

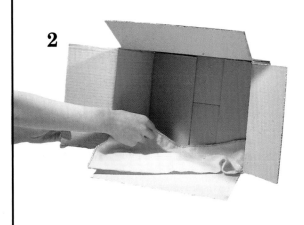

4

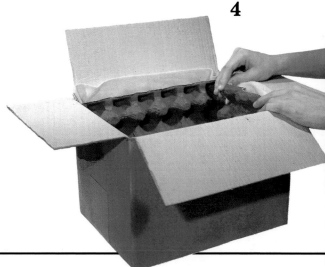

5. To test the soundproof qualities of your box you need a portable radio, or perhaps a portable alarm clock, a music box, or a toy that buzzes. Turn on your "noise-maker" and place it carefully into the box. Make sure it is something really noisy that you would normally be able to hear through the walls of a box.

5

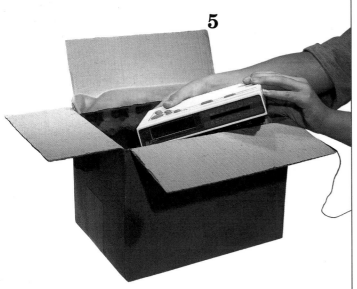

6. Insert your final layer of insulation and close the lid of the box. Notice what has happened to the level of the noise. The intensity of sound is measured in decibels. The quietest sound people can hear is about 20 decibels, and the loudest they can stand is 120 decibels. How many decibels do you think your soundproof box has cut out?

6

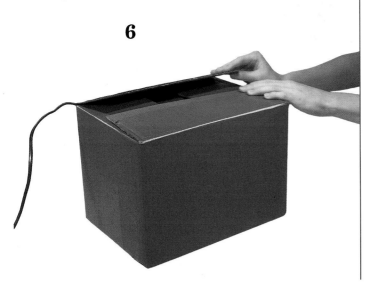

WHY IT WORKS

Your box stops the sounds of the radio in two ways. First of all, the soft materials that the egg carton and the towel are made from, are poor transmitters of sound. They do not vibrate and do not cause reverberation. Second, there are no solid, flat surfaces inside the box for sounds to echo or bounce off. Instead, the uneven surface of the egg cartons absorbs the sound, weakening it. The acoustic qualities of the box prevent the energy of the sound from escaping.

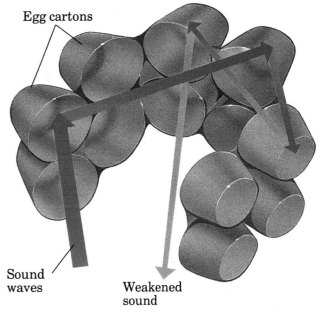

Egg cartons

Sound waves

Weakened sound

BRIGHT IDEAS

☀ Materials that stop sounds from traveling are called insulators. Experiment with different materials to find good and bad insulators. You could try styrofoam tiles, carpet squares, newspaper, wood, and so on.

☀ Call to someone through a window. Can they hear you? Try this again through a double glazed window – is it easy to hear? The space, or cavity, between the two panes of double glazing helps to insulate and keep out noise.

☀ Can you make yourself some noiseproof earmuffs?

☀ Do you have a toy that buzzes, like a wind-up train? Wind it up and let it go on a table (lay it on its side so it doesn't roll away). Listen to the noise. Now insulate it by standing it on a soft cloth or dish towel. Has the noise been lessened?

ORCHESTRAL SOUNDS

How many of the instruments in an orchestra can you name? Each one you can think of produces a different sound. Violins, cellos, and double basses have only four strings that vibrate when the musician moves a "bow" over them. Inside a piano there are many wires of different thickness that produce their sound when struck by small "hammer." The wires respond by vibrating, although the loud sound does not come from them directly. The vibrations spread to the body of the piano which makes the sound louder. In wind instruments, such as the flute or clarinet, the air inside the instrument vibrates and produces the music. There are three groups of instruments: percussion, which make a sound when struck, strings which are bowed or plucked, and wind which are blown.

SHAKE YOUR MARACA!

1. A popular percussion instrument is the maraca. Originally, maracas were made from hollowed out gourds, but you can make one of your own from papier mâché.

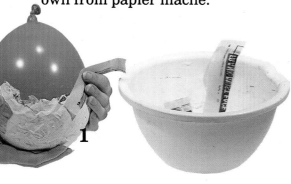

2. Smear a balloon lightly with cooking oil, then cover it with five or six layers of newspaper and paste. At the base of the balloon place a cone of cardboard with an open end.

3. Make sure that you overlap plenty of papier mâché onto the cone handle. When the whole thing is well covered, leave in a warm, dry place. After a couple of days, burst the balloon and remove it before painting.

4. For a lasting finish you could varnish your shaker. When dry, drop a handful of beans into it and seal the end with a cork or a piece of tape. Now you are ready to make your own music! (You can change the sound by using sand and rice instead of beans.)

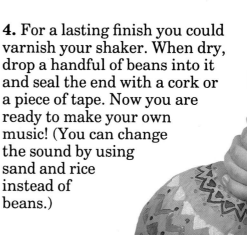

WHY IT WORKS

Whether plucking, striking, blowing, bowing, or shaking, a musician is using the same scientific principle to make the sound. When struck, the piano string and drumskin both vibrate, sending sound waves through the air. When bowed, the violin strings produce sound waves that reverberate around the sound-box and then reach our ears as music. And when you shake your maraca, the beans striking the papier mâché case cause vibrations that create sound waves again. The skillful musician knows how to produce the right notes.

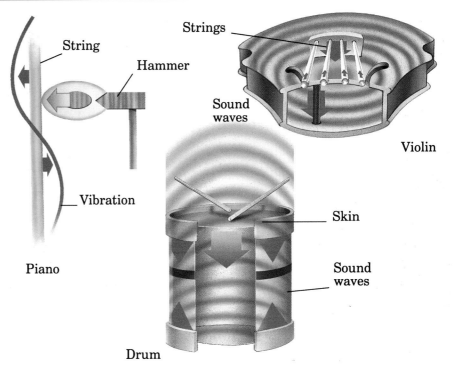

String

Hammer

Vibration

Piano

Strings

Sound waves

Violin

Skin

Sound waves

Drum

BRIGHT IDEAS

☀ You can make a "comb kazoo" by folding a small piece of wax paper over a comb. Put the comb and paper to your lips and blow. You should be able to feel the comb begin to vibrate.

☀ Ask an adult if you can put some water into a wine glass. Wet your finger and slowly rub it around the rim of the glass. You can produce a note.

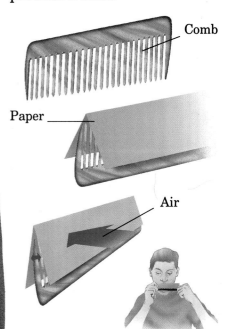

Comb

Paper

Air

FREQUENCY

Have you ever heard an organ playing? The notes that come from the larger pipes can be very low, while the notes from the smaller pipes are much higher. The higher pitched sounds have a higher frequency. Do you remember how a sound wave is made of expansions and compressions of air? One compression and one expansion is called a cycle. An object vibrating very quickly would have more cycles in one second. Scientists measure frequency in cycles per second, or hertz. One cycle per second is one hertz. A piano string that gives a high note vibrates at about 4,000 hertz. The lowest frequency that a good human ear can hear is about 20 hertz, the highest is 20,000 hertz. Radio and other frequencies are also measured in hertz.

BOTTLE XYLOPHONE

1. You can make a simple bottle xylophone. Find five bottles that are all the same and wash them well. Color some water with a little food coloring – this will make it easier for you to see what you are doing. Put different amounts of water into the bottles, as shown below.

1

WHY IT WORKS

The air inside the organ pipe vibrates and produces the musical note. In a large pipe there is more air, which vibrates slowly, making a low frequency sound. The small pipes contain less air, which vibrates more quickly, and the higher frequency of the sound waves sounds higher pitched to us. Your bottle xylophone works in the same way – where there is more water and less air to vibrate, the sound waves have a higher frequency.

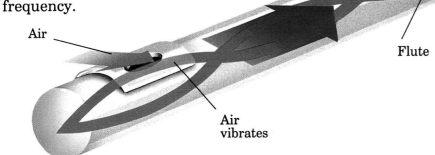

Air

Flute

Air vibrates

2. Stand the bottles on a piece of styrofoam or wool and make your musical sounds by tapping gently with a spoon or a wooden stick above the water line. To get a good range of notes you can alter the amount of water in each bottle. As an alternative, you can blow across the top of the bottle to make a sound. Can you play a tune?

2

BRIGHT IDEAS

Make some flowerpot chimes. Hang pots of different sizes and gently strike them with a wooden stick. (The pots must be clay ones, not plastic.)

Make your own set of tubular bells. You will need help from an adult here. Cut 6 lengths of copper pipe at 1.5 in, 3 in, 4.5 in and so on to 6 in. Tape a 12 in loop of string onto each one and hang them over a pole or stick. You can play the "bells" by hitting them with a spoon or stick.

Make notes with very high frequencies on your bottle xylophone. Find the highest note you can make. Do the same for low frequencies.

HIGH AND LOW PITCH

Notes with a high frequency have a high pitch, and it is the pitch of the sound, rather than the frequency, that we hear. The notes on the left-hand side of a piano have a low pitch – they are deeper sounds; those on the right are higher pitched. In a band, like a jazz band, different instruments tend to produce different ranges of pitch. A trumpet is higher pitched than a bass drum or a double bass. Notes with the same pitch can sound quite different though – a middle C from a violin is quite distinct from the same note of a piano. They do not have the same "tone quality."

PLUCK THAT BASS!

1. You can have a lot of fun playing your own version of a double bass. Here is how to make one. Start by finding a wooden pole about five feet long – an old broom handle would do. You can paint it with gloss paint.

1

2. Knot the end of a piece of strong string and attach it to the end of the wooden pole with a thumbtack or a small nail. Next you will need a large cardboard box – the bigger the better. Secure the lid down tightly and cut a hole 10 inches in diameter into the top.

2

3. Paint the box and then make a small hole in the top. Push the pole through so that the base rests on the bottom of the box. Carefully push a sharp stick or nail across the corner and loop a second piece of string around the ends, as shown on the far right.

4. Attach your string securely to the loop, and now you can play your double bass. Hold the pole and pull it away from the box to produce notes with a higher pitch. Relax your hold and slacken the string to make lower pitched sounds. Next, write your own jazz song!

3

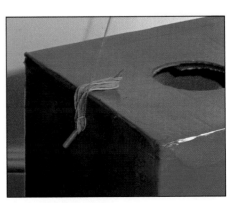

4

WHY IT WORKS

When you pluck the string in a slack state, it vibrates more slowly and therefore its frequency is lower. The top blue line shows a slow vibration with only two cycles. The note produced would be of a low pitch. When you pull the string tight and pluck it again, it vibrates more quickly and its frequency is raised. The bottom blue line shows four cycles in the same amount of time it took the top one to complete two. This would produce a higher pitched note. In actual fact, the high-pitched note of your double bass is probably vibrating at about 250 cycles per second. Therefore it has a frequency of 250 hertz.

Slow vibration

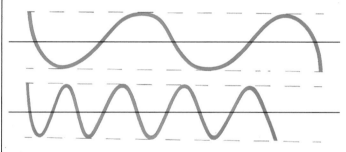

Faster vibration

BRIGHT IDEAS

☀ Try changing your double bass string for a thicker string, or fishing line, or wire. You will notice that the tone of the sound is different, although the pitch may stay the same.

☀ Turn on an electric fan and listen. At first the blades turn slowly and produce a low-pitched sound. As they speed up, the pitch gets higher. This is because the fast spinning blades vibrate at a higher frequency.

☀ Make a cookie tin guitar by stretching rubber bands around a tin that has its lid removed. You can loosen and tighten the bands to change the pitch of the sounds you make.

☀ If you have a guitar, pluck a string and then tighten and loosen the tuning keys at the same time. The pitch of the note will change as the tension of the string changes. Don't tighten the strings too much or they may break.

SPEED OF SOUND

Have you ever watched a thunderstorm? You see the flash of lightning, then wait to hear how loud the clap of thunder will be. In fact, both happen at the same time. You see the flash first, however, because light travels at 186,000 miles per second, a lot faster than sound's 1,000 feet per second. The sound of thunder travels one mile through the air in about 5 seconds – so a 10 second gap between the lightning and the thunder would mean the storm is 2 miles away. A very loud sound, like thunder, travels through air at the same speed as a soft sound, like a whisper. If the thing making the sound, like a fire engine's siren, is moving, however, the pitch of the sound appears to change. This is the Doppler effect.

WHY IT WORKS

By observing the time gap between seeing the balloon burst and hearing the bang, you have proved that sound travels more slowly than light. The Doppler effect happens because sound waves travel quite slowly through the air. As a fire engine comes toward you, the siren has a high pitch. The pitch will appear to fall as it moves past you and away. This is because the sound waves in front of the vehicle become compressed together as the fire engine follows behind. This causes a high-pitched sound. As the vehicle moves away, the sound waves become more spread out, leading to a lower pitched sound.

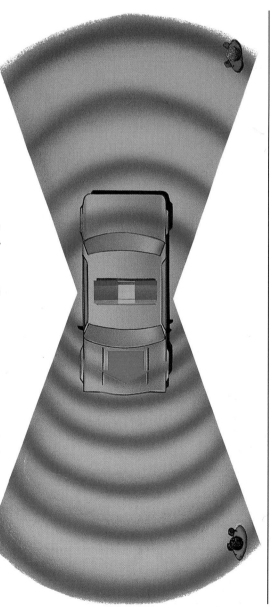

FLOUR BURST

1. Cut off the top end of a plastic bottle and fix a balloon over the spout. Secure the balloon with a rubber band.

1

2. Use the bottle as a funnel, and pour flour through it into the balloon. When the balloon is full, tie the end securely.

2

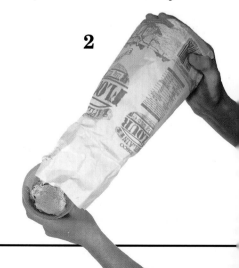

3. Hold the balloon of flour in front of you, and ask a friend to watch from about 150 feet away. The distance needs to be quite large, to distinguish between the bang and the flour burst.

4. Now take a pin and burst the balloon in one motion. Your friend should be able to see the cloud of flour before they hear the bang of the balloon bursting. This is because light travels to your eyes more quickly than sound reaches your ears.

3

4

BRIGHT IDEAS

Ask your friend to stand 300 feet away from you when you burst the balloon. The time gap between the bang and the flour burst should be longer. At 150 feet it should have taken 1/7 of a second for the banging sound to arrive. At 300 ft, the sound should take 2/7 of a second to reach your friend's ears.

Find out about the sound barrier. Supersonic airplanes like the Concorde break the sound barrier, causing a "sonic boom." This happens when the plane travels so fast it overtakes its own sound waves.

Next time you are in a big cave or a deep valley, shout loudly and listen for your echo. Time how long it takes to return. Do you think it would take longer to come back across the valley or the cave?

CHANGING WAVELENGTHS

Have you wondered how it is that an instrument, like a flute, can produce such a large range of different notes? The flute, like a clarinet or an oboe, is made basically of one tube. By blowing across the flute, the musician sets the column of air inside the tube vibrating. By pressing the keys, the size of the air column is changed – when it is shortened it vibrates more quickly, and so has a higher frequency. Because of this, the length of the sound wave (or wavelength) is shorter and the note has a higher pitch. Do you remember the organ pipes and bottle xylophone on pages 20/21? Can you see how those work in a similar way, as the amount of air is altered by adding water?

PANPIPES

1. For the pipes, use plastic drinking straws – the wider straws are much better than the thin ones. As an alternative, you could use plastic tubing or even hollowed out bamboo canes. You can buy these from gardening stores, as they are often used to support plants.

2. Cut the straws into 7 or 8 lengths, starting with 1 in and adding on 1 in for each pipe. Cut out two wedge shapes of corrugated cardboard (the kind used for sending packages through the mail is perfect). Arrange the straws so that the top ends that you will blow over are level with each other. Glue the straws into place making a sandwich with the cardboard. Trim the straws afterward if necessary.

3. Your panpipes will look very effective if you decorate them with paint. Glue two extra strips of cardboard along the top and bottom of the cardboard sandwich for extra strength. When you play the pipes, keep your head still and move the pipes, as you would with a harmonica.

WHY IT WORKS

When you blow over the pipes, you will notice how the longer ones create a lower pitch. The longer column of air vibrates more slowly when you blow

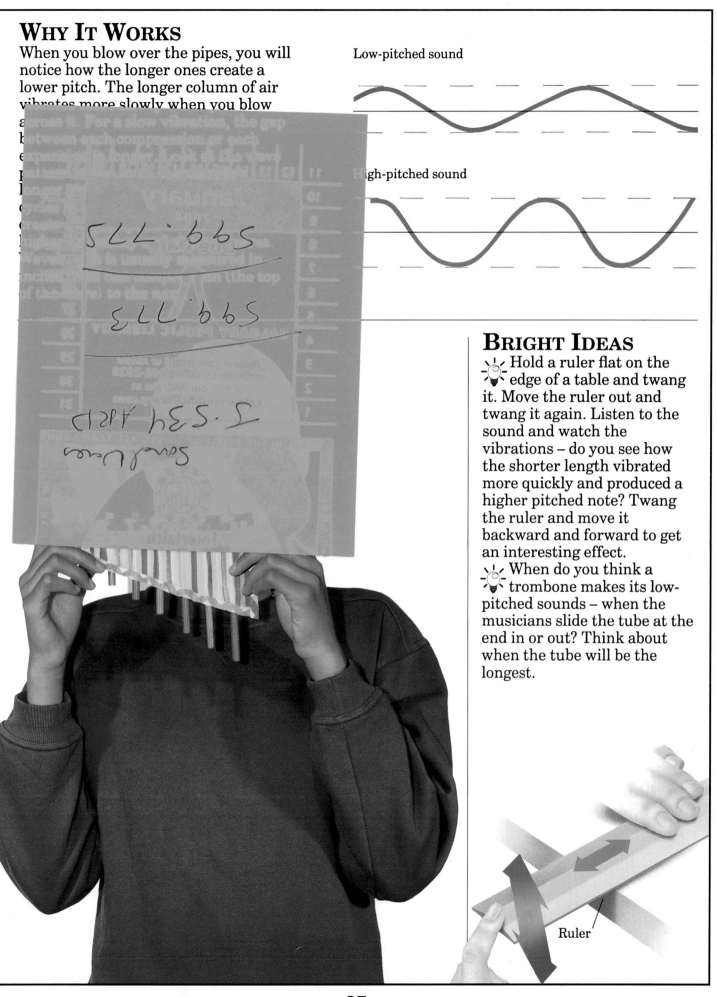

Low-pitched sound

High-pitched sound

BRIGHT IDEAS

Hold a ruler flat on the edge of a table and twang it. Move the ruler out and twang it again. Listen to the sound and watch the vibrations – do you see how the shorter length vibrated more quickly and produced a higher pitched note? Twang the ruler and move it backward and forward to get an interesting effect.

When do you think a trombone makes its low-pitched sounds – when the musicians slide the tube at the end in or out? Think about when the tube will be the longest.

Ruler

FUN WITH SOUND

Some of the most difficult instruments to play in the orchestra are the reed instruments, for example an oboe or a bassoon. The reed is held to the musician's mouth and blown to make the reed vibrate. An inexperienced player, though, can blow and blow without getting a sound from the reed! Organs, too, create their sounds by blowing through reeds, though in this case, the air is pumped through by bellows. Originally, reeds were made from the reeds that commonly grow by the edge of water.

WHY IT WORKS

When you blow, the tips of the reed vibrate. This sets the air inside the straw vibrating too, which transmits sound waves to our ears. Inside the tube there is a column of air that also vibrated in response to the vibrating of the reed. You can vary the length of the column of air depending on where you place your fingers. The larger the column of air, the slower the vibrations and the lower the pitch of the note becomes. Compare this to the bottle xylophone on pages 20/21.

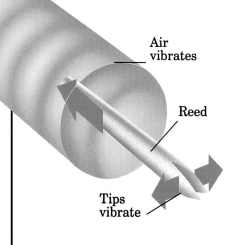

Air vibrates

Reed

Tips vibrate

REED SOUNDS

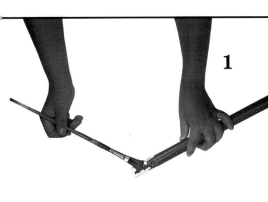

1. Begin by finding (or making) a tube of cardboard or oak tag. It needs to be about 20 in long and 1 inch in diameter. Paint your tube and leave it to dry.

2. When dry, carefully mark out the position of the finger holes of your reed instrument. Start with the first hole about 6 inches from one end and continue along the length of the tube. Make the hole with a sharp pencil.

3. Next, make the reed – you will need a 4 inch length of plastic drinking straw or art straw for this. Squash the straw flat at one end and cut a 0.5 inch piece from the center outward toward the edge. Repeat on the other side.

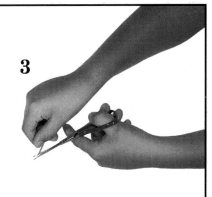

4. Place a cork or stopper in the end of the tube that has the finger holes. Next, practice blowing the reed. Place the squashed end into your mouth so that the cut parts are just inside your lips. Hold it lightly and blow gently.

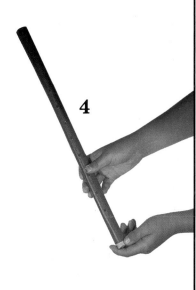

5. If at first your reed makes no sound, carefully open out the cut flaps so that they are just a millimeter or two apart. Try again. By making very fine adjustments to this gap, your reed will eventually work. When it does, put the end of the reed into the tube and change notes by covering different holes.

BRIGHT IDEAS

Make more reeds. Change the length of the reeds and find out whether longer reeds played on their own make notes with a lower pitch. Make a cone of oak tag and place it on the end of your reed. It will act as an amplifier, making the sound louder.

Put the end of a hollow tube into a bowl of water and blow across the top. Move the tube up and down, so changing the amount of air inside it; what do you notice about the pitch of the sound?

You can turn your reed pipe into a flute! Make another, larger hole 4 in from the end. Make the first finger hole, 2 in from this, larger too. Now hold the pipe sideways underneath your mouth and blow across the first hole to create a flutelike sound.

STORING SOUNDS

Storing sounds so that we can play them back is very big business today. It is possible to buy musical recordings on compact disks read by laser beams, on magnetic or digital audio tapes, and on vinyl records. The very first "record players" played back music recorded on wax drums, but the sounds were rather faint and very crackly by today's standards. Old-fashioned "gramophones" are easy to recognize – they have a large cone that is designed to amplify the sounds from the records. When a record is made, electrical signals cause vibrations and cut a groove in a plastic disk. When this is played back, vibrations in the stylus are converted back into the original signals, producing a sound. You can make your own simple gramophone.

SPIN A DISK

1. Turn three identical bottle tops upside down and stick them to the top of a cardboard box as shown.

2. Inside the bottle tops place a small piece of plastic straw. Make sure your "bearing" sticks up and out of the top and turns freely. Position the tops carefully so that a thread spool can be attached to the corner of the box when the record is in place.

3. Make a turntable from cardboard. Once it is in the right position, push a sharpened piece of a stick into the boxtop. As you see here, the box can be decorated.

4. To amplify the vibrations of the needle, make a large cone from a sheet of thin cardboard or stiff paper. Start off with a semicircle shape to give a neat finished cone. Glue it securely.

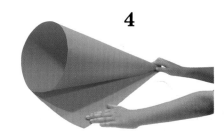

5. Stick the cone down to a cardboard disk and then carefully push a sharp stick through the cone and the center of the cardboard. Next push a dressmaking pin or fine needle through the end of the cone so that it faces down from the disk.

6. Now firmly push the stick through the spool on the corner of your box and through the top of the box. The disk should rest on the top of the spool.

BRIGHT IDEAS

Do the cone and the needle move across as you turn the record? If not, grease the top of the thread spool to reduce friction. Spin the record fast to create faster vibrations – do you notice how the pitch of the music goes higher?

Experiment with larger and smaller cones. Draw the needle over other rough surfaces – what sounds do you make? WARNING!!!!!! Do not use any records that you want to play on a record player again as your home made gramophone will damage them! Use only old records.

WHY IT WORKS

Inside the grooves of the record the surface is not perfectly flat. It is designed with a special rough surface which makes the needle vibrate as it travels along the groove. The vibrations of the needle alone would produce sound waves almost too quiet to hear, but the cardboard cone and the air inside it are made to vibrate too, and this makes the sound louder – it amplifies it. The acoustic qualities of the cone would be changed if you used plastic instead of cardboard, or substituted the whole thing with a cookie tin. This is because different materials have different resonant qualities.

Stylus

Grooves in record

Vibrations

Needle

7

7. Finally, you will need to balance the cone so that it is stable – you can see a green weight in the picture doing this job. The needle should rest on the record lightly. Now turn the record by hand and listen to the music!

Scientific Terms

AMPLIFY To make sound louder.

AMPLITUDE The range of a sound wave. The greater the wave, the louder the sound.

DECIBEL A unit of measurement for the loudness of sound.

DOPPLER EFFECT The way a sound changes pitch as it moves past you. It is named after an Austrian scientist called Christian Doppler.

ECHO The reflection of a sound.

ECHOLOCATION Using echoes to detect the distance and direction of objects.

FREQUENCY The number of sound vibrations per second, measured in hertz.

PITCH The highness or lowness of a sound, depending on the frequency of sound vibrations.

RESONANCE When a sound makes another object produce a sound because it has the same frequency of vibration.

REVERBERATION The bouncing of sound waves within a small space.

SONIC BOOM A loud bang from the shock waves created by an object moving faster than the speed of sound.

SOUND MEDIUM A substance that carries sound waves.

SOUND WAVES A regular pattern of pressure changes in solids, liquids, or gases, such as air.

SUPERSONIC Faster than the speed of sound.

ULTRASOUND Sounds with a frequency over 20,000 hertz, which are too high for people to hear.

WAVELENGTH The distance between the same point on any two waves, such as from the top of one wave to the top of the next.

Index